Blackbirds

G E O R G E ᴋ. P E C K

SMART APPLE MEDIA

Published by

Smart Apple Media

123 South Broad Street

Mankato, Minnesota 56001

⚜

Copyright © 1998 Smart Apple Media.

International copyrights reserved in all countries.

No part of this book may be reproduced in any form without

written permission from the publisher.

Printed in the United States of America.

Photos by George K. Peck,

Jeffrey Rich, Michele Warren, Joe McDonald/UNIPHOTO,

Richard Day, Rick Poley/Hillstrom Stock Photo, Inc.,

Bates Littlehales/Animals Animals

Editorial assistance by Barbara Ciletti

Library of Congress Cataloging-in-Publication Data

Peck, George K.

Blackbirds / written by George Peck.

p. cm.

Includes index.

Summary: Describes the physical characteristics, behaviors, and habitats

of various blackbird species.

ISBN 1-887068-14-7

1. Blackbirds—Juvenile literature. [1. Blackbirds.] I. Title

QL696.P2475P435   1998   96-19423

598.8'81—dc20   CIP

                                                                  AC

First Edition   5 4 3 2 1

CONTENTS

S ing a song of sixpence,

a pocket full of rye;

four and

twenty blackbirds

baked in a pie.

Not all birds called "blackbirds" are true blackbirds.

The "blackbirds" in this Mother Goose rhyme were a type of thrush. In America, the birds we call blackbirds are members of the Icteridae family.

Not all members of the blackbird family are black.

The Icteridae family includes 97 different species of birds, from the yellow-breasted Meadowlark to the bright orange Northern Oriole. Of these 97 species, about 40 are mostly black in color. These are the birds we commonly call "blackbirds."

Not all black birds are blackbirds.

Just because a bird is black does not make it a member of the blackbird family. Two of the most common black-colored birds in North America—the crow and the starling—are not true blackbirds—no matter how black they look. You can't always judge a bird by its feathers!

The Icteridae family is native to the Americas. Most blackbirds prefer the tropics, but there are 11 species of blackbirds that live and breed in the United States and Canada. Because there are so many different kinds of blackbirds, this resourceful bird family can be found in a wide variety of habitats, from the northernmost forests of Canada to the steamy coasts of Florida and Texas. No matter where you live, you are sure to have a few blackbirds for neighbors.

The Red-winged Blackbird, our most common blackbird, is found throughout the United States and southern Canada. During the summer months, Red-winged Blackbirds are often found near freshwater marshes, lakes, and rivers. The Tricolored and Yellow-headed Blackbirds also live around fresh water. The Boat-tailed Grackle likes water too, but it prefers the saltwater marshes along the southeastern coast. The Common Grackle chooses to live in open woodlands and in cities, whereas the Rusty Blackbird makes its home far to the north, in Canada's cool evergreen forests.

The four species of blackbirds known as cowbirds avoid forested areas in North America. They are called cowbirds because they frequent open pastures—just like cattle! The Brown-headed Cowbird is a common sight on farms and ranches across the United States.

A Common Grackle perched in an evergreen in Ontario.

Some bird families are very specialized. Ducks and geese have bodies built for living and feeding on the water. Hawks have claws and sharp, hooked bills designed for capturing and devouring small animals—a hawk wouldn't know what to do with a sunflower seed! Hummingbirds' long beaks and tongues are made for sipping nectar from flower blossoms. Woodpeckers have special beaks and feet that allow them to walk up and down tree trunks, hammering holes in the wood when they hear a tasty insect hiding inside.

Blackbirds are not so specialized. They are multi-purpose birds that live in many places and eat many different things. You won't find any giant blackbirds the size of eagles, and there are no tiny blackbirds the size of hummingbirds. Most blackbirds are average in size—about the size of a robin. The smallest North American blackbird, the Brown-headed Cowbird, is 7 inches (18 cm) long. The Great-tailed Grackle is bigger—up to 18 inches (46 cm) long—but half of its length is its tail!

In general, blackbirds have long, pointed wings. Their legs are made for walking instead of hopping, and they have sharp, cone-shaped beaks. The blackbird beak is a multi-purpose tool. It can shell a sunflower seed, snatch a buzzing fly from the air, spear an unlucky beetle, or—in the case of the Great-tailed Grackle—crack open an acorn.

Most blackbirds look mostly black.

But a closer look shows some surprising colors. The male Tricolored Blackbird has a bright red-and-white patch on each wing. The Red-winged Blackbird has a red-and-yellow patch. The male Yellow-headed Blackbird shows off a head and chest of brilliant gold. The females of these species tend to be less colorful. The female Red-winged Blackbird is a smaller brown-and-cream striped bird. If you don't look closely, you might mistake it for a large sparrow.

On a cloudy day, male grackles appear to be solid black, but when the sunlight strikes their feathers, they shine blue, bronze, and purple! This type of reflected color is called iridescence. You can see the same effect when you look at a sheen of oil floating on water. Common Grackles and Great-tailed Grackles also have bright yellow eyes, making them quite colorful for a "black" bird!

Female grackles look much like the males, but their iridescence is not as noticeable and they are smaller—the female Great-tailed Grackle is only two-thirds the size of the male.

The Brewer's Blackbird looks a lot like a grackle, but it is smaller and has a shorter, thicker bill. The males have yellow eyes and iridescent feathers, and the females are a duller blackish-brown color. Its close relative, the Rusty Blackbird, is the same size and shape, but it has rust-colored tips on its black feathers in fall plumage.

Good

B L A C K B I R D S

The male Brown-headed Cowbird has a blue-black sheen to its small body and, as its name indicates, a brown head. The female is gray-brown across its back and tail, with a paler breast area. The Bronzed Cowbird, a species found in Texas, Arizona, and Mexico, has similar coloring but is slightly larger and has a longer bill.

Swallows eat only insects. Hummingbirds live mostly on flower nectar. The pelican's diet is fish and more fish. Finches and cardinals want almost nothing but seeds.

Blackbirds are not so fussy. Blackbirds will eat insects, grain, fruit, or just about anything else that looks like food and is small enough for them to swallow.

Grackles are the least particular of all. They will dine on everything from frogs to acorns to other birds' eggs. They are notorious thieves, and are attracted to parks and picnic grounds where there is plenty of food to be found. You might even see a grackle fly off with a whole hamburger bun in its beak!

Cowbirds prefer insects for dinner, although they will not refuse a bird feeder full of seed. Red-winged Blackbirds are very fond of rice, wheat, and other grains. As many an angry farmer will tell you, a flock of Red-wings can eat up a lot of grain!

Brewer's Blackbird eating a minnow in Yellowstone.

Blackbirds are strong fliers, able to travel at more than 30 miles per hour (48 kph). Red-winged Blackbirds have a wave-like, up-and-down flight pattern. Grackles fly in a straight line, using their long tails as rudders.

In the spring and fall, blackbirds gather in flocks to migrate. In the fall, before the snow falls in the north, they fly south to avoid the cold winter winds. Some species travel as far south as Central America. In the spring, they fly north to their breeding grounds. Rusty Blackbirds fly as far north as the Arctic Circle to breed.

In the winter, Red-winged Blackbirds form huge flocks. They like to be around other blackbirds. Sometimes they are joined by grackles and cowbirds. One winter flock of blackbirds in Virginia contained 15 million birds—so many birds that when they took off the sky turned black. That would make a lot of blackbird pies!

Once the blackbirds return to their northern breeding grounds in the spring, they quickly establish nesting territories and choose their mates.

In late February or early March, the male Red-winged Blackbirds arrive, a few days before the females. They choose their territories, usually in wetland areas or shrubby pastures. The males sit atop the highest cattails or shrubs. With a shrill *o-ka-leee*, they announce to one and all that they have claimed an area as their own. Any other male blackbird had better stay away—the Red-winged Blackbird will defend its territory with its sharp beak and claws.

When the female Red-winged Blackbirds arrive, they must choose a mate. The male performs a courtship display. He spreads his wings and tail and raises his body feathers to make himself look bigger. He erects his bright red shoulder feathers, singing *o-ka-leee* over and over again. If the female likes what she sees, she might do a little dance of her own! If the females outnumber the males, some males might end up with more than one mate.

Every blackbird species has its own courtship display. Although blackbirds are not known for having beautiful voices, the males give it everything they've got during courtship. Their calls range from the Brown-headed Cowbird's squeaky gurgling to the creaky cry of the Common Grackle. The Great-tailed Grackle's "song" is a loud, piercing *may-reee,* and a high-pitched squeal: *quee-ee, quee-ee!*

Of course, the male blackbirds don't care what humans think of their songs. They just want to keep other males away.

Female Red-winged Blackbird in the marshes of Sanibel Island, Florida.

Once the females choose their mates, nest building begins.

The female Red-winged Blackbird builds a nest on the upright stalks of dead cattails or tall grasses. She uses coarse grass and strips of cattail leaves, then lines the inside of the cup-shaped nest with fine, soft grass to protect her eggs. Most Red-winged Blackbird nests are only a foot or two above the ground.

Grackles and Rusty Blackbirds prefer to build their nests in evergreen trees. Their nests are made from sticks and twigs, with softer grasses lining the inside. Boat-tailed Grackles look for a tree with a view—their nest can be as high as 80 feet (24 m) above the ground.

Cowbirds are one of the few birds that do not make a nest at all. Cowbirds are a traveling species. It has been theorized that for hundreds of thousands of years, cowbirds followed the bison herds across the American prairie, feeding on insects that were stirred up by the thundering herds. Because they were always on the move, the cowbirds lost their nest-building skills. Instead, they began to lay their eggs in other birds' nests and leave them there for the other birds to raise. Birds that use other birds to raise their young are called brood parasites.

Cowbirds are not particular about whose nest they invade—robins, warblers, sparrows, or other blackbirds—it's all the same to the cowbird. They usually lay only one egg per nest, but a single female cowbird may lay dozens of eggs in a year—each one in a different nest. The Brown-headed Cowbird has been known to parasitize 220 different bird species. It is important for cowbirds to spread their eggs around because some host birds will not accept a cowbird egg. Robins, Eastern Kingbirds, and Cedar Waxwings will roll the cowbird egg out onto the ground. The Yellow Warbler simply builds a new nest right on top of the old one, then lays a new clutch of eggs. But many other species— such as the Red-winged Blackbird—don't seem to notice that they have acquired a strange egg.

Most North American blackbirds lay clutches of two to seven eggs. The female Red-winged Blackbird lays one egg per day until she has a clutch of two to six eggs. The exact number of eggs depends on the age and health of the mother and the amount of food available. Red-winged Blackbird eggs are a beautiful pale blue-green, with black, brown, and purple speckles and streaks around the large end.

After the eggs are laid, the mother blackbird sits on her nest, keeping the eggs warm and safe by covering them with her body. This is called incubation and it helps the baby blackbirds grow inside their eggs.

In 11 to 14 days, the baby blackbirds peck their way out of the shells. Their eyes are closed and their bodies are covered only with a bit of fluffy gray down. A baby blackbird knows how to do just one thing: open its mouth for food! For the next two weeks, the mother blackbird is kept very busy. She brings them insects, spiders, and even snails. The babies never seem to get enough to eat. They eat their own weight in food every day. Sometimes the male blackbird helps feed the babies if he has only one mate.

Red-winged Blackbird babies grow quickly on their rich diet. By the third day, hard cases called feather sheaths appear on the baby blackbird's body. Inside these sheaths, tiny soft feathers are growing. By the end of the first week, the babies' feathers have come out of the sheaths. Around the tenth day, baby Red-winged Blackbirds have most of their feathers. Since the babies are much larger now, they hop out of the nest and perch nearby. They still cannot fly or feed themselves, and the mother is more busy than ever finding enough food for her family.

All blackbird babies are able to fly by the time they are three weeks old. Young Red-winged Blackbirds quickly venture off on their own, and their parents may set out to raise a second family. Common Grackles do not get rid of their young so easily. Baby grackles will follow their parents around for weeks begging food.

Cowbird babies tend to dominate their host nests. They usually hatch sooner and grow more quickly than the other babies. They get most of the food, and the other babies often die from starvation. But sometimes the situation is reversed: if a cowbird egg hatches in the nest of an American Goldfinch or some other seed-eating bird, it will not survive. The goldfinch feeds its young seeds, not insects. In this case, it is the baby cowbird who will starve!

During the first summer, young blackbirds—both male and female—look like small, plump versions of their mothers. By September, they have molted, or shed, their juvenal feathers. The new feathers make them look more like their parents, with the males showing the glossy black or colored feathers of the adult. By the following spring they are full-grown adult birds, ready to raise families on their own.

A blackbird can live for as long as 18 years. But the average blackbird will survive only two or three years in the wild. Like all wild creatures, blackbirds face many dangers. Many die before they ever leave their nests, killed by wind or rain, or by a hungry snake, raccoon, or even another blackbird! Some birds are killed by storms during migration. Even on a beautiful, cloudless day, an adult blackbird risks its life. It could be struck by a car, or fly into a window, or be snatched in midflight by a Sharp-shinned Hawk. For a bird that weighs only a few ounces, the world is a dangerous place.

To a blackbird, the most dangerous creature of all is the human being. When a farmer sees a cloud of thousands of blackbirds landing in his fields, he worries that all his hard work will be gobbled up. Many blackbirds are trapped, shot, or poisoned by humans trying to protect their crops. Some grain might be saved by killing birds, but most of the blackbirds' diet is insects, including corn borers and other crop pests. If it wasn't for blackbirds, we might lose more of our crops to insect invasions. Also, much of the grain eaten by blackbirds is waste seed left behind after the harvest. In the long run, blackbirds might be doing us more good than harm.

Blackbirds are also in danger from new construction in wetland areas. Red-winged, Yellow-headed, and Tricolored Blackbirds depend on wetlands for food and breeding space. When people invade these areas, draining swamps and spraying pesticides to kill mosquitoes, they are taking away the blackbirds' food and shelter.

With their noisy calls and large appetites, blackbirds are not always appreciated by people. But they remain an important part of our natural world. Even the Brown-headed Cowbird, with its parasitic ways, fills an important niche in our ecosystem.

The world would be a poorer place without the wheeling flocks of blackbirds filling the sky each spring and fall, the glossy, iridescent grackle doing his courtship dance, or the joyful sight of a Red-winged Blackbird, singing *o-ka-leee*, perched proudly at the tip of a waving cattail.